Title Page

Paranormal

Activity

What are YOU dealing with?
Ghost or Spirit? Angel or Demon? Or?

Written by: Geralyn St. Joseph

see www.WholisticUniversity.org for more about the author

Mahalo for your purchase!
Blessings! Geralyn St Joseph

Cover Art by Kenny Testa.

ISBN-13: 978-1502421944
ISBN-10: 1502421941

Dedication

This is dedicated to my mother, Tinker Bell, who taught me two of the most important lessons of my life.

You don't know what you don't know, so never believe that you know everything about anything.

And

The evil creeps in and you don't even know it's there.

These two lessons have shaped my lifelong journey of discovery about spirituality. She taught me to be ever vigilant and to never be so cocky as to believe you are invincible.

She is an amazing, powerful and wise woman. I am blessed to be one of her loved ones. Thanks mom for always standing strong for me, forcing me from under your skirts to make me stronger and being the tender nurturer you are when I was fragile. You always seem to know just how hard or soft you need to be with me, I am a strong woman thanks to you.

Acknowledgements

I accomplish what I can through the gifts of Spirit. It is only through the grace of God that I continue. Thank you God!

Much Mahalo [Thanks] to my friends and family who support me in my endeavors.

More specifically, Mahalo to Sue Nolan for encouraging me to write a book like this for as long as I've known her.

Thanks to *Kaleea* for her great feedback, I am sure her suggestions made the book much better. She let me know that I *wasn't* done.

Mahalo to *Syd Vitale*, my partner and love, for his proofreading and consistent encouragement.

Thanks *Ed* for keeping a comfortable roof over our heads so I have a dry place to work.

Mahalo *Dell*, without you I have no reason to write. I love you all!

Blessings! Geralyn

"God is a Spirit" John 4:24

Table of Contents

Other Titles:
Psychic Self-Defense for EveryOne – Why You
Need It & What You Need to Know
5 L's of Parenting
50 Ways You Can Change the World – Small
Steps for Making the World a Better Place

Coming Soon!
Things That Go Bump In The Night –*A Parent's
Guide to Empowering Your Child Against The
Darkness*

What's This All About?
This Psychic's World

Being who I am, I am often assaulted with the urgent questions – Am I crazy? What's happening to me? There have been quite a few times that I have urged people to seek medical help. More often than not, some therapy with the right practitioner is amazing. I always tell a person to try to find someone who is understanding, open and compassionate. You need to find someone who you are comfortable with. I prefer the counselors at Unity churches as they typically have a broader knowledge of the Spiritual than most secular therapists.

That being said, we live in a time when the veil* that separates dimensions is becoming quite thin. You may have heard the expression 'the veil between Heaven and Earth', which is the veil of which we speak. Why is it thinning? From what I understand, the dimensions are converging and eventually we will again collapse into the all that is. No need to worry about that now, nothing you could or would even want to do about it. How do I know this is happening? I am a scientist at heart; so much of what I know is through observation, direct experience, experimentation and asking the right beings, the right questions.

*The term 'veil' is actually a misnomer, however as it is used almost universally, for the sake of brevity we will use it here.

The most important intelligence that we deal with on a daily basis is the Universe, the all that is, the Source, God or as I like to refer to this being, Spirit. When I refer to Spirit with a capital S, it is God to whom I refer. My experience of God is as pure, unconditional love flowing through me and through all of creation. God is in all things and is all things. Jesus and many prophets came to teach us how to experience the God within us. I have studied several sacred texts, most extensively the Bible [I was raised Catholic] and the same basic messages are everywhere. But that's for another discussion. I experience Spirit as an essence; I hear its voice and consistently feel its presence. Everyone is capable of experiencing this. I can teach you how [but not in this book].

I don't want to be too complicated. I just want to let you know that as this occurs, even those who consider themselves to have no sensitivity will experience bits of the other side. I have been teaching people about the beings who share our world, but not our dimension, since I was a child. I was born with a close connection and tie to Spirit. This relationship has developed over time like any family relationship or close friendship.

Some people use the term spirits to encompass all non-physical beings. I won't do that. I see using such broad terminology somewhat demeaning. We are all animals, but each species is unique and deserves to be acknowledged for its individuality. The same is applicable to the unseen world.

The term spirit with a small s refers to people and other 3 dimensional living things that have crossed over into the Godhead. A spirit is a fully actualized entity that no longer has the hang ups it had as a physical being. As a spirit a consciousness can multi-locate, they see the possible futures and can assist in guiding you into a more fruitful potential. They have more control over their appearance, so often appear to those who knew them as being healthy and happy, regardless of their manner of death.

From what I can see in my experience working with young children, everyone is born with an awareness of Spirit. It is as we grow and rely on our parents and other adults for information that this awareness is taught out of us. One of the worst injustices we impart on our children is to dismiss their fears. We lie to them and tell them that monsters don't exist. Even if we don't believe in the other side, even if we don't believe in demons or fallen angels, there are monsters, they just may be human.

In the field of metaphysics there is no real consensus of terminology. What I mean is that each person uses the same terms in a slightly different way. So when you are speaking to a practitioner they should be able to give you a definition of their terms. If they can't they may be inexperienced or just simply uneducated themselves. I would like to educate you about Angels, Spirits, Ghosts and Demons; what I have experienced and what these terms mean in a more detailed explanation than you will receive from most people.

Many psychics and mediums don't have experience with multiple types of entities or don't realize it when they do. Discernment is one of the spiritual gifts listed in the Bible [I Corinthians 12]*. I believe it is a gift that can be learned. Let's see if I am right... or maybe not. It may not be the safest thing to do, proceed at your own risk.

Note
Throughout the book you will be presented with Bible quotes. If you are not Judeo-Christian in background feel free to skip them. The quotes I use are for enrichment, so their exclusion does not detract from the information given.

I do not assert that everything in the Bible is inspired, but I do feel that most of it was. There is quite a bit of good spiritual information that can be attained by reading the Bible books in their entirety, instead of just hearing quotes taken out of context. I suggest reading the entire passages I, or anyone else, quote to you to give you a better understanding of the meaning.

Reading the Bible with awareness is the key to understanding the true message. When you read the Bible you will find that it contradicts itself many times. There are 2 reasons for this that I can discern. The first is that some of the information, laws, advice, etc is meant for a specific time period or situation. A similar occurrence is found in the Koran in their war passages vs. the peace passages, the war verses were written in response to very specific situations the prophet was experiencing at the time. The second reason for these discrepancies is the interjection of another voice, an uninspired voice. So when the tone of a passage suddenly changes, take note and open your heart to Spirit so that you can discern the imposter.

I prefer to use the *Amplified Bible* for my quotes because I find it easier to read and multiple interpretations are given for words that can be interpreted in various ways. This gives you the ability to read the story in context and decide which interpretation is most relevant.

> * "12 *Now about the spiritual gifts (the special endowments of supernatural energy), brethren, I do not want you to be*

misinformed.

4 Now there are distinctive varieties and distributions of endowments (gifts, [a]extraordinary powers distinguishing certain Christians, due to the power of divine grace operating in their souls by the Holy Spirit) and they vary, but the [Holy] Spirit remains the same.
5 And there are distinctive varieties of service and ministration, but it is the same Lord [Who is served].
6 And there are distinctive varieties of operation [of working to accomplish things], but it is the same God Who inspires and energizes them all in all.
7 But to each one is given the manifestation of the [Holy] Spirit [the evidence, the spiritual illumination of the Spirit] for good and profit.
8 To one is given in and through the [Holy] Spirit [the power to speak] a message of wisdom, and to another [the power to express] a word of knowledge and understanding according to the same [Holy] Spirit; 9 To another [[b]wonder-working] faith by the same [Holy] Spirit, to another the extraordinary powers of healing by the one Spirit;

10 To another the working of miracles, to another prophetic insight ([c]the gift of interpreting the divine will and purpose); to another the ability to discern and distinguish between [the utterances of true] spirits [and false ones], to another various kinds of [unknown] tongues, to another the ability to interpret [such] tongues.
11 All these [gifts, achievements, abilities] are inspired and brought to pass by one and the same [Holy] Spirit, Who apportions to each person individually [exactly] as He chooses." 1 Corinthians 12(AMP)

A Ghost, A Haunting, An Emotional Imprint or a Poltergeist?
What is happening here?

I Thought This Was a Quiet Neighborhood

Every night at 3am you wake up to the sound of music, followed by the sounds of a heated argument. The first half dozen times you flew out of bed, checked the house, yelled at the neighbors, only to realize that the sound was coming from...where? You might be able to see it, or just catch glimpses from the corner of your eye. What are you dealing with?!?

I want to begin by explaining certain phenomena that does not have consciousness. Not having consciousness means that it cannot interact with you or its environment. The first phenomenon is what is called an emotional imprint. An emotional imprint is created when an emotionally charged event takes place in a space. This can be accomplished by a similar impression being left a multitude of times in the same area over a long period of time, such as a slaughter house, or a wedding chapel or hospital. Or it can be the imprint of one major event, such as a battle, or a murder suicide.

Places like Gettysburg and Valley Forge have emotional imprints from the battles and the torment of the men who fought and died there. In

Philadelphia you can sometimes see glimpses of Ben Franklin hurrying around center city.

These emotional imprints are like stubborn stains on the energy. They tend to hang there and are very difficult to remove. The most noticeable emotional imprints are comprised of intense negative emotions, like rage, fear or sorrow and are sometimes confused with a ghost or a haunting. Emotional imprints aren't always negative, however. They can be formed by intense love, loyalty, joy and devotion also. We just don't tend to notice those quite so much.

Have you ever been in a place where you just feel really happy or peaceful? Maybe a wedding chapel or a room in the house, somewhere that people experienced joy on a regular basis. This is an emotional imprint.

Sometimes these emotional imprints play like a movie. They repeat a slice of life. These can often be heard and at times even seen. The players in these scenes cannot interact with their current surroundings since this is just an after image and holds no consciousness.

It seems like every time you have an argument with your teen, something breaks. It's not that they throw stuff or do anything you can put your finger on, but something always breaks. Pictures fly off the wall, their stereo [do these even exist anymore?] starts to go crazy, a glass is cracked…inside the cabinet! What are you dealing with?!?

The second phenomenon is poltergeist activity. A poltergeist is a 'noisy ghost', this of course is a misnomer since a poltergeist is seldom found to be a conscious ghost. Although a vengeful ghost can become rather rambunctious and be noisy this is seldom the case. Much poltergeist activity is actually attributed to an excessive energetic. There is often a very hormonal individual, such as a teen, at the center of poltergeist activity. We do not know the full capabilities of our brains. As our brains develop there are times we have excessive energy, often caused by hormonal shifts and intense emotions. Most poltergeist activity resolves over time.

> Many years ago, I had a family come to me who had the problem of things flying off the wall and off shelves whenever there was a family dispute. It didn't seem to matter who was arguing. They thought it was the house they were living in that was haunted, so they

moved. Moving did not solve the issue, in fact, it was getting worse. We investigated the house and met with the entire family. I sensed no outside entity, but I did feel a great deal of power.

I interviewed each family member and eventually figured out that the young son was the common denominator. He did not like it when there was any fighting and it caused him to become very upset. Even as we spoke about it he began building energy around him. I brought this to his awareness. He was under ten years old, but understood. We practiced feeling his energy and holding it in a containment field so it didn't do any damage.

I suggested that he learn a variety of coping methods such as meditation, counting backwards, deep breathing etc. for the most part the poltergeist activity stopped until the boy hit full puberty. Being aware of his energetic field allowed the boy to have more control over the events that occurred due to his emotions, and thus allowed him to live more peacefully.

Although both of these phenomena can be noisy, poltergeist activity can actually disturb physical objects where an emotional imprint cannot.
Another way to discern between these two types of activity is frequency of disturbance.
An emotional imprint is a lingering feeling; it is there ALL the time. When it plays a random slice of life scene of great emotional intensity it tends to happen consistently – the same time every day, or every year for example. In contrast, poltergeist activity is often sporadic and unpredictable.

**There are many other definitions of poltergeist activity also. Some use the term to simply explain any noisy commotion or physical evidence of the paranormal, like moving objects, cabinets and windows opening and closing. The term poltergeist is sometimes used as an adjective to describe a type of activity [i.e. noisy or with movement] as opposed to using the term to describe the source of the commotion. Since this book is more about discernment, and heavy activity like those mentioned above are indicative of particular entities, we use the definition of poltergeist activity as an unconscious phenomenon.

Dead, But Not Gone

You keep feeling like someone is watching you, seeing something out of the corner of your eye and suddenly you feel really sad, but there's no reason for it. It seems that the lights keep flickering when you enter the room, but you checked them all. They aren't loose and there is no electrical problem. What are you dealing with?!?

Speaking of spirits always brings up the issue of ghosts. Ghosts are also disembodied souls, but these have not crossed over. They cannot bi-locate and often choose to remain in specific physical confines, for reasons I will explain later. Ghosts do not know the future or future potentials any more than you do. They are simply people without a physical body. These bodiless people tend to retain and even exacerbate their hang ups. They often appear as they looked at death, but not always. They do learn as their existence as a ghost continues. And it will continue until they are released in some way.

I don't buy into the belief that ghosts have unfinished business or that their lives ended prematurely. I have met just as many ghosts who lived into old age without incident as murder and accident victims. What creates a ghost really has nothing to do with the nature of their demise. It has far more to do with their beliefs. The movie Ghost was pretty accurate in its portrayal of the portal and the confusion that comes with sudden death.

What I have learned is that when most of us leave our physical confines we are met by a guide. This can be in the form of a relative, loved one or angel. There are times when there is more than one. We often begin seeing these guides shortly before passing. This guide helps us in our transition. For many there is a period of 2 to 6 weeks where we remain Earthbound. We do this to make sure our loved ones are okay and, let's face it; we all want to see who shows up at our funerals.

Let me be clear here. Our physical bodies DO NOT need to be laid to rest before we cross. Once we leave our physical confines we are done with them, barring any dark magic that may bind us, or a part of us, to them. That's a whole different story, and something we don't really have to worry about in our modern world since most of that knowledge is gratefully lost.

A ghost can be created in a number of ways. As I said, I do not buy into the notion that a ghost has unfinished business. I don't buy into that because the majority of ghosts I've come across have been in that condition for a very long time. Whatever business they may have thought they had is long gone.
The most common reason I find for the

creation of ghosts is fear, specifically religious in nature. In short, people are taught to fear the 'punishment' of the afterlife. They are afraid of going to hell and their fear condemns them to be bound to the Earth indefinitely.

Another cause of a soul being Earthbound is a loved one who refuses to let go. When our loved ones pass, we need to let them. Release them from any promises or commitments that they made to you. Let them move on and meet God rejoining the Godhead to experience the fullness of their being. This also aids you in your mourning process and creates space in your life for love to flow freely.

A ghost is a person without a physical body. Imagine being aware of everything around you, everyone around you and not being able to interact with any of it. You see your loved one crying and you can't comfort them. To be aware and unable to communicate effectively, to have those around you react to your presence with repulsion or fear and not be able to let them know your story; if that's not hell, I don't know what is. These poor souls are trapped. Their primary emotions are fear, anger, frustration, anxiety and extreme sorrow. That realization is a heavy one.

Over time ghosts can develop skills that allow them to manipulate electrical devices. The most common effects are making lights flicker, ringing telephones [this seems more prevalent with older phones], changing TV channels, turning electronics off or on and draining batteries. Ghosts most often take things in a natural direction. For instance they will close a window since it takes much less energy than to lift it. All they need to do is create a vibration to loosen the window and gravity does the rest. They may manipulate physical things in this way. Some can even learn how to manifest but this is rare. [When I say manifest I mean to come into physical or near physical form.]

Sometimes a ghost will allow you to see it. This may be an individual thing; they only allow *you* to see them. Or they may make themselves visible to whoever may be looking. Oftentimes their appearance is accompanied by strong emotion.

A ghost is not really stuck in a physical location – fear keeps them in place. Imagine if you choose to believe that life is normal, but you see everything happening in the outside world, and you lived for 100 years. How much has your neighborhood changed in the last 100 years, 20 years, or even 10 years? Can you imagine how it would feel if you wanted to believe it was always 1982, but you saw what was happening in the outside world? Isn't it easier to maintain your denial if you only had to deal with one room, or one house? This is why a ghost will choose to stay in a location. When the soul leaves the body it will usually return to a place the person was comfortable and stay there.

Some ghosts will attach to a person. This can be a person they know, or someone who looks similar to a lost loved one. Or can it simply be someone who can see or sense them. Again, a ghost will attach to a person or thing that is comfortable for them.

Ghosts tend to gravitate to those who can sense them, so people who are naturally sensitive will seem to have more experiences than those who are not. The auras of certain people are attractive to ghosts also. They are like a lighthouse guiding them into the light. The issue with this is that most of these people don't know how to open a portal to release the ghost. I enjoyed the depiction of this in the movie 'Ghost Town' [2008].

Many ghosts end up wandering on the streets after being 'cleared' from their homes. I found out early in my career that it was unusual to ask what happened to the ghost or entity once you cleared it from a space. No one seemed to know, or care. I was also given a great deal of misinformation, like that a suicide victim was sentenced to purgatory/earthbound for a certain number of years. I discovered that if you simply clear an area you are just pushing the ghost from its familiar place, in essence making them homeless. They will then wander until they find somewhere else to be.

> There have been many times I
> find my car suddenly filled with
> 'people'. One of the most
> memorable groups of ghost
> hitchhikers was two women and a
> man; a wife, her husband and his
> mistress. Imagine being stuck in
> that trio for a hundred years or so!
> The wife shot the couple mid-tryst,
> then turned the gun on herself.
> This trapped these three good
> Christian folk mid sin. Hence they
> were stuck for many decades, living
> in the same spot. The house
> changed over time and eventually
> a new owner had the house
> cleared. The trio was forced onto
> the street. Left to wander until
> they jumped in my car shared
> their story and found passage to
> heaven.

One thing that I find interesting is that a ghost
will often 'hibernate' for periods of time. There
seem to be long periods of inactivity that are
broken by some event. This event could come in
the guise of remodeling the house or room they
'rest' in, or playing with an Ouija Board,
anything that creates an energetic or physical
disturbance in the area.

The *Ouija Board* is the commercial name for the talking board. Actual talking boards come in many styles and can be found as either rectangles or circles. Similar devices and ways of communicating with the unseen have been around since ancient times. A planchette, or device used for automatic writing, was one such device. The concept behind these styles of 'spirit' communication is to summon a nearby entity to answer questions.

The issue I have with this type of device is that there is no discernment when calling in the entity, so there is no veracity to the information given. Also, by 'summoning' an unknown entity you may be inviting something nasty into your life.

When 'Mary' was awakened by the girls playing with the Ouija board in their room at college, it was their parents who suffered. Over the next ten years the parents of girls who lodged in Mary's room received hysterical phone calls from a girl pleading for forgiveness and saying she didn't mean it. Needless to say, this was quite alarming. The frequency of the calls lessened over the years following the playing of the Ouija Board and stopped all together when we crossed Mary over in 1994.

Mary was just a ghost, but more sinister elements can be called forth with the Ouija also. When you are inviting something to play, know who and what you are inviting. The consequences can be dire.

Ghosts, and most non-physical life forms, do not have the same concept of time that we do. During one of the first ghost/possessions I was called upon to clear the ghost told me that she'd been in the house for 10 years, when in fact she had died over 60 years previous. I surmised that she was in 'hibernation' in the house until her rest was disturbed with the use of an Ouija Board.

One of this particular ghost's main complaints was being 'played with' as if she was not a conscious 'living' person. It made her very angry when people treated her like a game, asking her to repeat an action over and over again. She was the ghost of a 19 year old, suicide victim and she demanded respect. Once we understood her plight she calmed down considerably.

When a ghost contacts you it is often to ask for help. They get really excited when they are acknowledged as the human consciousness they are. Imagine being ignored for a few decades, then suddenly having someone speak with you. Wouldn't that be exciting?

A ghost most often presents as cold, it may be a cold spot, or draft. Their presence will raise the small hairs on your body, and sometimes give you goose bumps or chicken skin. If you are at all sensitive, you may experience a sudden, irrational surge of emotion. This happens when they are very close and trying to communicate with you. The emotion will center above the nose, between the brows, often experienced as pressure. DO NOT express the emotion, do not cry or yell, or do anything you suddenly feel compelled to do. By accepting the emotion, you are accepting the ghost into your physical being.

A ghost entering your physical body is called possession. Most ghosts and people in general don't realize that taking on the emotion is allowing another being into your physical space quite literally. What I am saying is that it is not usually a malicious act on the ghost's part, more of an accident, but if neither of you knows what you are doing it can be quite dangerous.

A possession, especially where two souls are vying for the same physical body, will result in the degradation of the body. Our physical bodies were not created to house two souls and can't handle that kind of energy on a consistent basis.

This is why most people who channel entities [allow another entity, or life force, to enter their body and use it to communicate] become frail and sickly over time. The most common negative effects on the human body are seen in our nervous systems through disruption of the electrical impulses that rule our bodily systems. Heart failure is a very real consequence of a long term possession, or battle for a physical body.

The first possession I had to deal with was with Mary entering a college student in 1994. It was interesting and scary at the same time. The possession was off and on for three full days. I learned a lot about ghosts in those three days. Someday I will publish the whole story. Suffice it to say that I was thrown into my vocation by this event. It made me realize the plight of ghosts, and that the ghosts were not the only things going bump in the night.

Now that we know what ghosts are and how they are suffering, what do we do?

Ghosts are mostly harmless. You can live in a haunted location indefinitely and very peacefully, especially if you have good rapport with the ghost[s]. They are just like any other roommate, who doesn't pay their share of the bills, but doesn't usually make much of a mess either. They also don't eat your food.

A ghost *will* on occasion take items and hide them from you. Remember they are simply disembodied people, so they have similar motivations. They may also be able to help you find things that you've lost, if you ask. A ghost can also warn you of a present danger. Remember, they do not see the future so their information is limited like yours. However, they can be the 'fly on the wall' and pick up more information than you can. That can be helpful.

I think that most people have the ability to clear a ghost. Other types of entities are more difficult, and clearing is not without its concerns. The key is that the ghost needs to want to leave. They need to have faith that they will rejoin with God, or go to heaven. You can push them in that direction, however some can be really stubborn. At times you may need the assistance of God's Angels or a spirit who has crossed over and can reassure the individual.

Whether you chose to believe it or not, we all go to the same place when we are done here. We rejoin with the all-that-is. [Ecclesiastes 12:7*] I have come to this conclusion through study and observation. I have cleared murder victims and their murderers, adulterers, suicide victims and soldiers; they all go to the same end. I believe that being Earthbound should count as some kind of justice, it is definitely imprisonment.

> * 7 Then shall the dust [out of which
> God made man's body] return to the
> earth as it was, and the spirit shall

return to God Who gave it.
Ecclesiastes 12:7(AMP)

Once a ghost is cleared from the physical realm through a portal to heaven that must be opened, it rejoins with Source and becomes a spirit. It is easier for these spirits to communicate with us since they have access to the Astral plain and thus our dream time. Many of the ghosts I clear send me a message of gratitude and allow me a glimpse of their current state. I have also had ghosts that I cleared help me in times of need. I will describe spirits shortly.

We all go to God when our physical body expires. Part of our consciousness is embodied in the physical, while the rest is embedded in our souls. Our personality seems to be a soul piece so is retained after death. Our personality is an aspect of our being that differentiates us from the whole.

We are like the leaves on a tree; each different and unique while remaining a part of the whole. Each with its purpose and it's time for living as an individual, then it falls to the ground to be reabsorbed by the roots and taken up again into the tree.

Aren't You Supposed to Be in Heaven?

Your child keeps telling you family history they should not know. You ask them who told them and they tell you about meeting their grandparent. They describe in vivid detail what they look like and what they said. But their grandparent is dead. There's no way this could happen, right? What are you dealing with?!?

In much literature, including the many translations of the Bible, there are few, if any, distinctions made between ghosts, spirits, unclean spirits, demons and fallen angels. For example in many Bibles the translation describing possessing spirits is given as unclean spirit, evil spirit, defiling spirit, impure spirit, wicked spirit, bad spirit and at times simply demon. Which of these translations you see will depend on which version of the Bible you read. These terms may all seem pretty similar, and to a certain extent they are. However, dealing with an unclean spirit that was once a human is very different than facing a demon.

Truth be told, not many people have the ability to discern between these entities except in their most extreme forms. I will attempt to explain the differences and similarities here, some are very subtle.

As you know a ghost is a disembodied person, once this disembodied soul has crossed over and rejoined with source it becomes a spirit. A spirit can bi-locate. A spirit's consciousness is very much expanded once they have rejoined with source, the Godhead. They have a greater understanding of life and its lessons as they have access to the akashic records.

> The akashic records are the sum total of all knowledge. These records hold the history of all souls and all life on all worlds in all dimensions. Heavy, I know. Just think of it as an etheric library that our souls have access to so we can benefit from the lessons learned throughout time. It is a flow. Some believe that the records give us access to the future, since time is a man-made construct.

A spirit is more helpful than a ghost can ever be; they are more peaceful and more knowledgeable. A spirit usually will not manifest except under extreme circumstances, such as to warn a loved one of danger. When they want to communicate they generally do so through the astral plane – through dreams. If you are highly sensitive you are apt to see them. When a spirit communicates with you it is usually someone you know or an ancestor. Sometimes they share secret symbols with you, talk to you or allow you to feel their presence with a touch. I have a friend whose mother leaves him pennies in the most unusual places.

Note: Oftentimes children are greeted by the spirit of a grandparent who passed. My Nanny announces her presence with the scent of Jean Nate. She just likes to let us know she's around sometimes.

The Dead and the Restless

Every time you are alone the TV changes channels or turns on and off. Your pictures fly off your dresser, like someone angrily knocked them down. You feel like someone is watching you. You feel angry for no reason. What are you dealing with?!?

Then what is an 'unclean spirit'? An unclean spirit by my definition is a ghost who is driven by negative emotions and whose emotions of anger, frustration, etc can become overwhelming. They are more powerful than the usual ghost because their energy is much more focused. This is a vengeful ghost.

An unclean spirit tends to present more physically to get your attention and do things that frighten you, whereas your typical ghost is just starved for attention, preferring affection. An unclean spirit is considered unclean due to its negative emotional field, a field created by sin. To sin is to sever ourselves from God through our actions or by our words.

> To sin means to be separated from God. Ghosts by their very nature are 'living in sin' since their disconnect from Spirit and lack of true faith is what led to their being Earthbound. The field created by sin that I refer to above is more in line with the major, conscious sins

such as, murder, adultery, rage, lust, greed...basically the deadly sins.

These vengeful spirits want to be physical and have no desire or intention of crossing over. They will try to enter any human who will allow it. How does one allow it? By consciously opening ourselves is one way, as in opening our field to channel an entity. Doing this for a specific entity leaves us open and vulnerable to other types of beings, especially when the host is empty during the transition of souls.

Most students of channeling do not know how to completely close and heal their aura after they rip their auras open and submit to their voluntary possession, leaving them susceptible to whatever is in the neighborhood on a fairly consistent basis. I have seen a variety of entities use a channel when the channel only thinks there is one. If you watch, listen to or read different channels you will notice a change in tone, diction or message at times. The invasion is usually subtle, but if you follow your own intuition you can feel it if you are paying attention.

Other more common ways to invite an entity into your physical body are through alcohol or drug use. You know that feeling of being 'buzzed' where it feels like your eyes are floating above your eyes, you feel yourself hovering. That's your soul detaching from your physical body. It is very easy to knock a soul from its body in this condition.

Some people only use the term spirits to refer to strong alcoholic beverages. Think for a moment that the term spirit is from the Latin 'spiritus', meaning breath. The breath is associated with the soul/life energy in many cultures. Spirit also means to swiftly steal or take away.

Now I am going to tell you a secret. There's a reason why many belief systems discourage drinking alcohol. It CAN be a sin; you can most definitely lose your soul. Most people drink responsibly, they don't drink to the point of blacking out. Most people don't have severe personality changes, at least not after just a glass or two. BUT, some people do. For some people, and I am not just talking about alcoholics, some people undergo severe personality changes when they drink. Some people experience lost time and blackouts. This is dangerous for more than just the obvious reasons.

Know anyone whose personality drastically changes when they drink? The drinker's whole presence changes, there is an energetic shift. They have problems remembering what they did or said while intoxicated. When you are intoxicated your soul can easily be pushed out of your body. If you drink regularly, there are entities who hang out in your energy field just waiting for their next opportunity to jump into your meat suit and strut around wreaking havoc on your life.

Self-abuse or any type of abuse that injures the self-esteem and/or the physical body will cause the aura to be weak and also allow entry to any entity that might be hanging around. The entity/unclean spirit will cause the host to have cravings that continue the cycle. The continued use of a substance will create a physical addiction. Once this happens, it is a hard cycle to break and takes both self-control and spiritual strength.

The difference between a simple ghost and a vengeful ghost/unclean spirit is that the latter have an agenda. That agenda is to control you in some way. They prefer to control your physical body through possession, but will settle on controlling you through anxiety and fear by being a pest. These unclean spirits are only as strong as you allow them to be. They can only enter if invited. The problem is that most people don't realize when they have issued an invitation.

A very interesting case that I handled early in my career was brought to me by the friends of a gentleman who had undergone a major personality change after the death of his mother. Shortly after her death, 'Gerald' began drinking heavily on a regular basis. Several of his friends noted that his personality changed to that of his mother when he drank.

She apparently was a very harsh, judgmental woman, in contrast to her son's gentle, almost meek, nature. His friend's were shocked at his transformation. Another clue was the fact the man was not a drinker before his mother's death. He had a few drinks after the funeral which was the opening his bitter mother needed.

She invaded Gerald's body and began changing his life. She was particularly hostile to the friends she disapproved of when he was alive. At the times when Gerald was sober he knew something was amiss, he was having stress dreams about his mother destroying his life. His friends brought me in to talk to him and wouldn't allow him any alcohol. Mom was NOT happy and showed her displeasure through the electrical systems, flickering lights, ringing the phone and turning the TV on and off. This was a bit unsettling for Gerald.

Once I cleared his mother, not without a fight, Gerald and his friends were very relieved. Gerald went back to being a non-drinker. Once Gerald's mother was crossed over, she realized her mistakes and wanted to make amends. His mother came through in a subsequent reading and apologized for her selfish behavior.

Now that we know that a restless ghost can invade our bodies, what do we do to prevent it from happening to us?

My advice is to be more aware of your surroundings and your actions - don't indulge in too much alcohol, no hallucinogens or unnecessary drugs [you can garner the same feelings of being 'high' from deep meditation], be aware that with any physical injury there is an energetic injury that also needs to be healed. And most importantly, nurture your sense of self-esteem.

To remain clean and clear of any type of entity possession, one must maintain a strong energetic. How do we do that? We cleanse our energy regularly using prayer, meditation and good, clean living. Let Spirit flow through your heart regularly and there will be no room for anything else. We are most content when we follow our soul's calling. Do what you love, treat others the way you wish to be treated, and most of all be kind to yourself.

Check out these podcasts on your Spiritual Journey: http://www.blogtalkradio.com/geralynstjoseph

The Trouble With Demons

*You feel uneasy when you are home, like
someone is watching you and wants to hurt you.
You have severe headaches that seem to
dissipate as soon as you leave the house. You
had the house checked for environmental causes,
but there's no mold, or fumes the inspector can
find to explain your pain or illness. Things seem
to move, you keep finding your wedding pictures
on the floor. Then you wake up with 3 deep
scratches on you. Now it's time to worry. What
are you dealing with?!?*

Ghosts, unclean spirits, vengeful ghosts and
such are easy to rid yourself of, not so for many
other beings. One of the biggest issues in
dealing with a vengeful ghost is the creature
that is usually feeding on it. That would be a
demon. Demons are non-physical life forms that
feed off intense emotion, especially appetizing is
fear. Another favorite is sorrow or misery. These
creatures prefer easy pickings, so a frustrated
ghost is perfect since they will perpetuate their
own suffering.

Once the ghost, a.k.a. food source, is cleared, it
can spell trouble for whoever is left in the area. A
starving animal turns its attention to next most
convenient food source, which just might be
you. There will be inexplicable feelings of malice,
either towards you or from you. Remember the
favored food is fear, so if you feel stalked, or

react violently towards those around you; fear is elicited from the hosts. Either will work for your demon.

Demons come in many varieties, with a host of different talents and appetites. They range from mildly annoying to physically dangerous, the simply mischievous to the purely evil. The level of destruction is usually a good indicator of what you are dealing with as far as strength.

Wounds from this type of entity range from unexplained mild bruising to bleeding claw or teeth marks. A medium strength to powerful entity will produce physical scratches on the victims. The depth of the scratches seems to signify aggression. And the size of the wound, like figuring out the size of a shark by its bite mark, indicates the beast's size and strength. Generally the bigger the beast, the stronger it is. The action of scratching you seems to be the demons way of 'marking' you, like a lion scratching a tree to mark its territory, whereas, a bite is just the creature aggressively putting you in your place.

However there are those who don't show their full hand until they are threatened. Properly discerning the strength of the demon and never underestimating your opponent is essential for your survival and success.

I have also found that some types of demonic beings travel in packs, or small groups. Be careful of this as the most dominant is generally the one that presents as a manifestation, so the 'underlings' are often hidden until the leader is removed or threatened.

These under-beings are generally less self-sufficient. They are much easier to remove than the leader; however since they are in packs they tend to jump you all at once. Not a pleasant experience, I can assure you. It is always best to make sure you discern what you are dealing with before you tangle with it.

One case I dealt with in Hawaii Kai on the island of Oahu in Hawaii involved multiple layers of entities. It started when a family took in an old friend who was suffering from mild mental illness. After she moved into the household the children began experiencing events with a little girl. She was playful most of the time, but also seemed quite frightened at other times.

This was followed by sightings of a dark figure a few months later. Once the figure of a man was seen things started moving. Pictures were knocked off the wall, glasses were broken.

The family friend, who I will call Ellen, began spiraling into a depression. Medication did not help, so they turned to more holistic means of trying to treat the woman. The worse her condition became, the more active the 'ghosts'.

Eventually the head of the household called me in to figure out what was going on and what could be done. This was a multi-layered manifestation involving various entities.

First, we figured out that the little girl was actually a soul piece* of Ellen's. She was created when Ellen experienced a trauma as a child. We called her little Elly. We needed to integrate little Elly into Ellen's soul. We did this by performing a soul retrieval in which Ellen welcomed back that lost part of her soul.

Second, we had to clear the house and its grounds of the ghost figure. This was a man who also suffered from depression and had committed suicide. He was happy to go and crossed over easily.

The house was quiet for a short while and then the paranormal activity escalated. There was a demon present who had vacated the premises for the clearing. It hid itself until it thought I was gone for good, and then began to terrorize Ellen, and eventually the rest of the family. The activity seemed focused on Ellen, her fragile mental and spiritual state making her easy prey.

I returned to perform an exorcism on the house. The children were sent to a safe place and the adults gathered in the living room. We sat in a circle with Holy Rose Water in a bowl in the center of us. I instructed everyone to hold hands and not break free of one another no matter what happened.

We began the process fairly strongly and peacefully. Suddenly, one of the men was being choked. We saw his throat constricted and turning red. He was gasping for breath. We all held fast to each other. 'Use the holy water!' I ordered. The people on either side of him dipped their joined hands in the water and splashed his throat. He was immediately released.

The woman to my left yelped and a large welt appeared on her arm. The entity attacked each person in the circle as their resolve wavered. By the end of the process the entire family was bruised. This was a powerful beast. It took several hours to banish it from our dimension and put it to work elsewhere. Finally, the house felt light and Ellen felt free. We were all exhausted, but continued to bless the house with a final clearing to make sure there was no stray energy left.

The peace lasted for several weeks. Ellen was preparing to move and gathering her things. A TV was unplugged and placed on a table in the parents' bedroom. At 3am the TV turned on. Needless to say, this freaked out the entire family. They placed the TV outside the house. At 3am the TV turned on again.

This is an instance of the strongest demon being the only one up front. He had left his minions behind. I went back to the house to perform a final exorcism. This one took less than an hour, with no injuries. Finally the house was totally cleared.

There are also smaller, pack creatures that do not need an alpha to lead them. I refer to these smaller entities as wasps. They can be very annoying, and when en masse, physically disabling. They are very wispy, with a faint energetic signature. They tend to be very concentrated attacking specific areas of the physical body or psyche. The pain they inflict is very tangible whether physical or emotional, yet subtle. Like the feeling of a cold coming on, or short sharp pains in the neck or leg.

Energy healing, such as Reiki, seems to work well in dislodging this type of entity. White light meditation, smudging and rose or holy water is also very effective. These critters are persistent and profuse, so cleanse your energetic on a regular basis. If these remedies don't work, look for a different cause, maybe you *are* just getting a cold.

From my experience, demons seem to be multi-dimensional creatures meaning that they exist on and can escape to another plane of existence. They do not seem to be able to bi-locate, so where they are is where they are. This differentiates them from fallen angels and spirits and puts their species more akin to ghosts in its abilities. This also means if it's in your room and your child's room at the same time, you have an infestation problem.

Since demons can only be in one place at any one time, they cannot appear to two individuals in different places at the same time. If you are seeing a demon in your room, while your child sees it in their room, you are not seeing the same demon. There is more than one. From my experience, if you see two there are probably 3 or more. As I mentioned above, there may be a primary demon with minions, or it can be a group of equals.

A demon will most often present as a foul smell, a dark figure and/or a disembodied insistent voice. A demon will use simple, effective ways to freak you out. Most demons can move and manipulate physical objects and will do so in a threatening manner. Things like slamming doors, breaking sentimental objects and turning electronic toys, etc on loudly are favorites. The aim is to startle the victim to push them off balance emotionally and elicit uncertainty and fear. The more fearful you become the more prone you are to physical attack.

The demonic being will seem to present to certain individuals, yet 'disappear' when certain other individuals are around. This can be for many reasons. From what I have seen they tend to do this to split the home and destabilize their victims. If it only appears to mom and the kids, chances are dad will doubt its existence and no one will try too hard to dispel it. This also creates yummy anger, frustration and anxiety in the environment.

If the victims become doubtful of the demon's existence they will feed him plenty of doubt. They will lower their energetic guard trying to convince themselves they are mistaken. This breaks down your faith, faith in God and in yourself making your soul easy and yummy pickings for even a low level demonic.

Note
I have had just as many cases that were not demonic at their source, so I suggest always talking to a knowledgeable psychiatric professional to discern the source of your disturbance. When the only evidence of paranormal activity is audio, there is a good chance you are suffering from a mental issue. Be safe, talk to a doctor you can trust. Tell them EVERYTHING you are experiencing so they can give you an accurate diagnosis. Blessings

The Downside of Demonic Possession

You feel indestructible and engage in risky behavior. You start craving things you never wanted before and saying things that seem to just jump out of your mouth. You find yourself being confronted by friends and family for things you don't remember doing. Your appearance undergoes subtle changes. You feel out of control. What's going on here?!?

At times, if you are particularly vulnerable, a demon will take possession of a human host. In this instance where the possession is made physical and the demon is in complete control of the body, the demon will feed on the host soul and the fear it engenders from those around it.

A person can become vulnerable to demonic possession in a variety of ways. They do not need to believe in demons for this happen. In fact, those who believe they are above reproach and are filled with spiritual pride are most vulnerable for long term demonic possession. Just because you look away from the bus about to hit you and pretend it isn't there, doesn't mean it can't kill you.

Being prideful, especially if it involves espousing a doctrine of hate that is attributed to a sacred teaching, is a grave sin. It disconnects us from the Love that is God and removes us from the true sacred teachings of grace and compassion. This spiritual pride fills us displacing our love of God, leaving no room for Spirit to flow through us.

Drinking alcohol, using drugs, injury, illicit sexual behavior, physical or emotional abuse, and channeling of entities opens our energy fields to invasion.

For the most part demonic activity is subtle and progresses slowly. It will often seduce the host to elicit an invitation. It may approach a child to play, or give companionship to someone who is lonely or depressed. Its actions seem quite innocuous at first and become more threatening as it gains power over the host. Long term demonic possession is extremely rare from my experience. However, a demon may hang out in the host's aura for years only entering the physical body on occasion.

Most demonic possession is short term, such as when a person is affected by alcohol or drugs. From my experience most demons seem to dominate an area and effect what they can in that space. They induce certain energetics in their chosen space which they use to manipulate the Earthbound souls and unfortunate living souls that happen to stumble into their presence. Torturing a family pet seems to be as satisfying as a person. Our pets frequently sense the presence of a non-physical entity long before we do.

A long term demonic possession often presents as an unfamiliar sense of strength. Someone with low self-esteem is suddenly standing up for themselves, this becomes very forceful. They seem able to convince others to do things out of the ordinary. The host will feel powerful as the demon orchestrates their life. There is often a false sense of security as the host achieves their goals with little effort and lots of charisma.

> I was once called upon to help a woman who had suffered a demonic possession for almost half her life. It began when she was a young woman practicing Wicca* and dabbling in the occult. She practiced channeling for a period of time.
>
> *Wicca is a nature religion that honors the Earth and all life. Wicca is not evil. Like all religions there are love based practitioners and those hungry for power.
>
> The she became addicted to drugs and alcohol. She had quite a

colorful sex life. Then she 'found' Jesus and sort of cleaned up her life. From the outside it looked different, however on the inside the insidious nature of the beast that controlled her was growing stronger.

She preached and taught the 'Christian' doctrine of exclusion and hate. She cultivated followers to her flavor of Christianity. Meanwhile she still indulged in drugs and alcohol; she simply did it in private. She no longer engaged in sexual promiscuity, rather insisted on being married...over and over.

In this case when I investigated the spiritual health of this individual I found an infestation. Not one, but seven demons inhabited her physical being. Her soul was ripped and tattered, unable to maintain her physical form. If I proceeded with the exorcism, she would die. So I stopped.

Preaching the Bible does not make someone a good person. Jesus the Christ said you will know them by their fruit. The path of destruction left behind this woman, the broken families and legacy of hate she espoused should be enough for any 'true Christian' to see through her guile. Unfortunately there are many out there just like her leading good people astray.

The host is often torn when confronted with the opportunity to discard the demon, as they believe that the demon has given them power. Also, the longer the possession, the less of the host soul exists. The soul becomes weak and tattered. Eventually, it is no longer sufficient to sustain the physical body; it is the demon's energetic that fuels the body at that point. Several demons can inhabit the same individual although this is rare for short term possessions.

> *'In conclusion, be strong in the Lord [be empowered through your union with Him]; draw your strength from Him [that strength which His boundless might provides]. Put on God's whole armor [the armor of a heavy-armed soldier which God supplies], that you may be able successfully to stand up against [all] the strategies and the deceits of the devil.'*
> Ephesians 6:10-11 AMP

Now that we know that demons exist, how can we protect ourselves from them?

A happy, well-adjusted, truly faithful individual

is not appetizing. My advice is to do what you can to be joyful. We all have moments of sadness, but when you live your life in an attitude of gratitude it is very difficult for these beings to get a foothold. Cultivate your spiritual nature by connecting with God, your own body and your energy field. Have faith, develop your talents and share them.

> *Faith*
> I want to discuss what I mean by faith for a moment. Faith is not the church to which you belong. Faith is a very personal, deeply ingrained connection to God. Our faith allows us to sense the Almighty. Faith drives us to seek out our connection to Spirit and to cultivate and nurture it. Faith is our internal instinct that either grows stronger in our acknowledgement or weaker in our doubt. Faith is that piece of Spirit that lives within us, the Christ within.

I do not want to engender blame in the victim for the possession. There have been some that I cannot explain how or why a certain individual was targeted, such as a toddler. When you begin to blame the victim, you feed the demon.

Spiritual Pride – Destroyer of Souls

You believe that anyone who is not the same faith as you is lost and deluded. You judge others harshly, yet make excuses for your own bad behavior. You take lessons and quotes from the Bible [or other sacred texts] without looking at the context to make your point. You think everyone who is spiritual is wrong. What are you doing?

Whenever we speak of faith we must consider the difference between true faith and bravado. Spiritual pride was mentioned often by Jesus the Christ as being the downfall of many. He warned us against taking that posture and also against following these false teachers who speak out of prideful motivations.

One of my favorite Bible passages is the Sermon on the Mount where Jesus lays out his instructions for us very clearly. Many pseudo-Christian churches espouse hateful rhetoric. They usually pick and choose passages from the Bible they decide to use out of context to support their blustery, hateful claims. In contrast to this Jesus the Christ taught:

> *'11 But he who hates (detests, despises) his brother is in darkness and walking (living) in the dark; he is straying and does not perceive or know where he is going, because the darkness has blinded his eyes.'*
> 1 John 2:11(AMP)

If you read this passage in its entirety you will discover that Jesus the Christ was very adamant about his followers loving one another and giving respect to all. We need to remember the foundation of Christ's teaching:

> '31 *And as you would like and desire that others would do to you, do exactly so to them.'* Luke 6:31 (AMP)

When we forget these simple laws we open ourselves to deception. We follow 'False Teachers' who try to convince us of their grandeur and that we need them to know God. But we know that anyone who teaches hate does not follow Christ and lives in darkness.

> '39 *He further told them [b]a proverb: Can a blind [man] guide and direct a blind [man]? Will they not both stumble into a ditch or a [c]hole in the ground?*
>
> 40 *A pupil is not superior to his teacher, but everyone [when he is] completely trained (readjusted, restored, set to rights, and perfected) will be like his teacher.'* Luke 6:38-40 (AMP)

Once you believe that you are above reproach you are most vulnerable to Fallen Angels and Demons. You let down your guard, lose your humility and feed them with pride. Even Jesus the Christ was beset by demons and tempted by the king of fallen angels [Luke 4:5-8], why would you be different?

Check out this podcast:
http://www.blogtalkradio.com/geralynstjoseph/201 0/12/12/spiritual- journey--what-makes-a-christian

> FYI – A good indicator of where a religious teacher is coming from is the way he/she refers to the Christ. When a church or teaching emphasizes Jesus and not the Christ, they are focusing on his human attributes, not the fully actualized Christ that Jesus was teaching us to evolve into. When a church teaches in a way that separates us from the Christ they are leading us to sin. Jesus the Christ told us all to follow in his footsteps, that we are ALL sons and daughters of God.

> "38 *John said to Him, Teacher, we saw a man who does not follow along with us driving out demons in Your name, and we forbade him to do it, because he [a]is not one of our band [of Your disciples].*
>
> 39 *But Jesus said, Do not restrain or hinder or forbid him; for no one who*

does a mighty work in My name will soon afterward be able to speak evil of Me.

40 For he who is not against us is for us." Mark 9:38-41 (AMP)

Fallen Angels vs Angels of God

You read a book and now you are ready to summon your angels. So you sit down and go through the process. You don't get a name right away, but you keep trying. Eventually you can really feel them and things are looking up. Your angels speak to you consistently. You get what you want, but then things seem to go awry. What are you dealing with?

Many people believe demons and fallen angels are the same things. I have not experienced that. Demons lack the intelligence and beauty of angels, fallen and otherwise. A fallen angel will come to your aid and gain your trust before beginning the torment. A demon is not so sophisticated. A demon will most often present as a foul smell, a dark figure or a disembodied insistent voice. A demon will use simple, effective ways to freak you out.

A fallen angel on the other hand takes pleasure in the cultivation of trust. Recently, many people who think they are communicating with the angelic host, especially Michael, are actually communing with a much more sinister entity. At times the exchange is innocuous, and others it can be downright dangerous. Misinformation is given, mixed with truth. They enjoy the confusion they cause with half truths.

> *'14 And it is no wonder, for Satan himself masquerades as an angel of*

light;[15] So it is not surprising if his servants also masquerade as ministers of righteousness. [But] their end will correspond with their deeds.' 2 Corinthians 11:14-15 (AMP)

Demons sometimes do consort with fallen angels. They act almost like con artists in a confidence game. The fallen angel will allow the demons into your energetic field so that you increasingly rely on the fallen angel. The demons get to feed regularly and the fallen angel gets to sweep in and 'save' you, earning your devotion. Eventually you become convinced that you need the angelic presence at all times to ensure your safety. In contrast, an angel of God dispatches the demon with permanence, unless you call the demon back into your field, which we will discuss later.

Another big difference between God's angels and the fallen angels is found in what they engender in you. A fallen angel will seek after your adoration. They feed off your love, gratitude and adoration of them. To gain this devotion they will try to give you everything you want. Attaining your goals and receiving things you want sounds good, but remember that what you want isn't always what you need. Sometimes getting what we want stops us from attaining what we need.

Remember in the film 'Bruce Almighty' the chaos that ensued when Bruce granted everyone their prayers? Morgan Freeman as God chides him explaining that people don't really know what is best for them. This is a fundamental truth. We can't see the big picture, so we don't have reasonable information to make a decision.

Have you been in a relationship that you struggled to hold together despite obvious issues that only became clear after the relationship was over? We pray, we beg, we plead for this one person thinking that they are the one, when in fact there is a better life after them. Or maybe you believe you need to follow a particular path to happiness, but it is in a totally different direction. Often times we can't even imagine what is in store for us. I have given dozens of sessions where a client is told of an opportunity that they believe is impossible. They fight it, argue with me and try to get me to change my guidance. Then a few months later I receive an astonished phone call telling me that it happened and how happy they are with the situation.

An angel of God will sometimes tell you NO very clearly. They may not tell you why, just know it is because it is for your greatest good. An angel of God seeks to bring you closer to Spirit. These angels do not propose to substitute themselves for Spirit. An angel of God is a conduit to Spirit, they are messengers. A fallen angel blocks your path, placing themselves between you and Spirit. A fallen angel will corrupt the message.

I received a phone call from a woman who said she was being tormented. She wasn't sure what was happening to her.

She read a few books on getting to know your angels and practiced the ritual for summoning her angels. In the beginning the angels told her their names – Ezekiel and Isaiah. These angels gave her much comfort and some good advice. This lasted for about a month, and then their advice started not working out so well.

They began waking her up at night to tell her urgent things. Things she found not to be worth waking up for. They wanted more time and more attention, constantly talking in her ear.

This constant barrage of misinformation, with a sprinkle of useful information took its toll. She began having marital issues. She was always exhausted. It was affecting her life.

She called me to investigate and I found that the entities were pretty strong and VERY attached to her.

In discussion I found that she was resistant to giving them up and had convinced herself that something was interfering with her communication with angels.

I explained to her what I saw happening and convinced her to try an exorcism/clearing to get some relief. We succeeded in releasing her from their hold and shielding her. This lasted about 2 weeks.

The activity came back in the middle of the night with a vengeance. They woke her up and kept her up. At this point I called my colleague, who lived closer to the client, to do an in person session with her. Shaman Christopher went to the woman and spoke with her and her family, and cleared the house. Again this worked for a while.

Ezekiel and Isaiah came back. I never had this type of issue before, what was happening? Upon talking to the client I discovered that she had continued trying to talk to her angels. Every time they came back, they were stronger and became more integrated with her being.

It was like a woman trying to recapture the first blush of romance in a relationship once it had gone sour. She was like an abused spouse who keeps returning to the marriage and trying to make it work. There was nothing I could do. I referred her to a psychiatric hospital in the area to help her deal with the underlying issues that were causing her attachment.

It is important to notice these differences since angels, both fallen and those of God, present the same way. They feel like a hot spot or sometimes will heat the entire room. The presence of Michael is known to heat the room as much as 20 degrees. I sometimes feel like my bones are on fire when Gabreal* gets too snuggly. I gently ask him to be a little less intense and he creates a more subtle impression.

*Yes I spelled that right. He prefers his name spelled that way.

Angels are often accompanied by a pleasant odor. They engender a sense of peace and calm. Angels are purely energetic beings, they have never been human. They can, however, manifest in human or animal form when necessary.

Grandma does not go to heaven and become an angel. She becomes a spirit who can in turn become a guardian or guide to you or yours. This is very different. Angels only have a sympathetic understanding of the human condition since they never experienced it. They know of us through observation alone.

There is one exception to this that I know of...

There are two reasons given for the fall of angels from heaven. The first is the desire of Lucifer to be adored. The second is the desire of some angels to be physical, to be human. I am aware of fallen angels who have chosen to become human. They are not as prideful or deceptive as those from the first group. No need to feel sorry for them as this is their choice. I do not know what becomes of them at death, although I would theorize that their soul is now human so their fate would follow that of a human.

What is an Exorcism?

In my vocabulary I use the term exorcism only when removing a demon from a person or location. I call it a clearing when dealing with ghosts and other energies. As you know, a demon is an entity that has never been human and feeds on emotions such as fear and anxiety.

In my experience you do not have to believe in demons to suffer a possession. Some of the things that make people susceptible are: physical trauma, any type of abuse that alters a person's perception of self, drinking, smoking and drug ingestion of any kind that alters one's energy and/or thought processes. I have also seen possession due to a karmic agreement by the person or a parent. Everyone is susceptible to a certain extent. It's more a matter of knowing your own Self and acknowledging when something isn't right. Quickly recognizing a stray emotion or negative thought gives you the power to refute it.

I find that people who engage in the type of religions that teach a lack of self-worth are feeding grounds for these negative entities. The Bible [Jesus the Christ specifically] preaches to love ourselves, so any church telling us how wicked and undeserving we are directly opposes the gospel. Letter of Paul to the Romans is full of warnings against such preaching pretending to be from God. Especially Romans 16: 17*. I'm not going too far into that. I have a Bible Study on Blog Talk Radio you can refer to if you are interested. Demons are not church specific or faith specific, however they will manifest in a way particular to the victim. Be strong in who you are, your faith and be joyful - demons hate that! Blessings!

Check out this podcast:
http://www.blogtalkradio.com/geralynstjos eph/2012/10/18/demystifying- exorcism-- what-it-is-what-it-is-not

> * '17 I appeal to you, brethren, to be on your guard concerning those who create dissensions and difficulties and cause divisions, in opposition to the doctrine (the teaching) which you have been taught. [I warn you to turn aside from them, to] avoid them. 18 For such persons do not serve our Lord Christ but their own appetites and base desires, and by ingratiating and flattering speech, they beguile the hearts of the unsuspecting and simpleminded [people]. 19 For while your loyalty and obedience is known to all, so that I rejoice over you, I would have you well versed and wise as to what is good and innocent and guileless as

to what is evil.[20] *And the God of peace will soon crush Satan under your feet. The grace of our Lord Jesus the Christ (the Messiah) be with you.'* Romans 16:17-20 (AMP)

Where do you suggest an individual go if they are looking for someone to perform an exorcism? Do most exorcisms require more than one person?

I would recommend finding someone who makes you feel deeply at peace when you speak to them. They should also try to rule out mental illness or other causes for your woes.

I was raised Catholic and I know that Catholic exorcisms are rarely performed. And honestly, a full blown exorcism is seldom needed.

How many people participate depends on the situation. I have done them alone with the subject or have had the family who is effected involved at other times. The key is that if it is a person who is infected, they need to truly want to be cleared and they must have faith that God will deliver them. Sometimes this is accomplished in the course of the work.

Some take weeks where others take only an hour. Every situation is different. Make sure whoever you hire is compassionate and not just flaming your fear to make as much money from you as possible.

They should know what to do with the entity
once they remove it so it doesn't come back.
They should instruct the subject to fortify their
connection with God and their protection to
ensure against a relapse. Family members and
those close to the subject should also be
protected during and after the ritual.

Does Lightening Strike Twice?

I mentioned earlier that after a demon is exorcised, even when the exorcism is successful, it can return. This happens when the host calls the entity back into their energetic space and/or the demon was not disposed of properly. First, one should not just 'clear' a demon and displace it. When this happens they wander around looking for another victim, or waiting for their host to become vulnerable once more.

> '43 But when the unclean spirit has gone out of a man, it roams through dry [arid] places in search of rest, but it does not find any. 44 Then it says, I will go back to my house from which I came out. And when it arrives, it finds the place unoccupied, swept, put in order, and decorated.
> 45 Then it goes and brings with it seven other spirits more wicked than itself, and they go in and make their home there. And the last condition of that man becomes worse than the first. So also shall it be with this wicked generation.' Matthew 12:43-45 (AMP)

Second, the host should be taught how to 'fill' their energetic space and strengthen their aura to prevent a relapse. Being possessed, whether

by a demon, ghost or other entity, creates tears
or holes in the aura. These need to be repaired.
Very similar to breaking a bone, when not
attended to properly these become weak spots
vulnerable to re-injury [or re-entry as the case
may be].

What ARE You Dealing With? - Discernment

In the past decades the popularity of angels has increased every year. There are numerous books about contacting them, communicating with them and asking for their intercession. All these texts make it seem so easy, so simple. I love the angels; I love all God's creation. However, not all God's creatures have our best interests at heart. There are those things that are put on earth to test us, to make us stronger and more defined.

Let us remember that there are 'fallen angels'. Lucifer was the brightest of the angels. What makes people believe that they can tell the difference between the angels they want and whatever shows up? Lucifer and his ilk are known as the great deceivers, it is what they do best.

Developing discernment is essential if you wish to entertain these majestic beings. Discernment is one of the spiritual gifts listed in the Bible [1 Corinthians 12]. When you put out the call for guidance, remember there are many layers of existence and many different types of entities that hear you. Typically, whatever are closest answers first.

How do you discern who/what you are talking to?

Discernment is definitely a skill that is learned over time. My advice is not to summon

ANYTHING if you do not know what you are doing. First and foremost you need to understand your own Self and be able to interpret your body's signals. You need to gain awareness, know your blind spots and your triggers.

It is always best to raise your own vibration before asking for assistance. This can be accomplished through meditation and prayer. Take a dip in the ocean or a sea salt bath/shower. Spend time with positive people, even if that means watching or listening to Wayne Dyer, Joel Osteen or the like.

Be ready to question whatever shows up. The rule of thumb is to ask questions 3 times to see if the answer changes. If they get perturbed when you do this, tell them to beat it, they are not an entity you want to deal with. The positive guides have patience and know the drill. Those that don't, can't help you anyway.

Test them by asking them about things you already know, and things that you will know the outcome of shortly. A ghost doesn't have any more info than you do [except as a fly on the wall], a demon can see emotion, intention and thought, but cannot see the future. A fallen angel can see the future, but will throw in some misleading advice after the third inquiry. I don't know why the number three is the key, but I have experienced that it is. Remember, third time is a charm.

If you have been working with the same guide for a time and their information suddenly seems less reliable, chances are you are communicating with someone different. If you listen too intently to an imposter, the truth is impossible to hear. I suggest creating a secret signal with your primary guide once you have established a solid connection.

To create your secret signal you need to clear your space of anything that does not belong there. You can do this using a white light meditation. http://wholisticuniversity.blogspot.com/p/pra ctices-for-spiritual- development.html

Set a sacred boundary and invite your primary guide in by name. Sense their presence and ask them to give you a secret signal. It can be something they present to you, or you can tell them what you want to see/hear/feel or taste when they come into your presence. Test it three times. Now every time they are with you, they will give you the signal so you know it is them. If something is communicating with you and it sounds/feels like them, but does not give you the signal, dismiss it.

Listen to this podcast: http://www.blogtalkradio.com/geralynstjoseph /2012/11/12/angels-demons-- know-who-or-what-you-are-dealing-with

Choosing a Good Psychic/Spiritual Advisor

Check out this podcast:
http://www.blogtalkradio.com/geralynstjoseph
/2010/01/31/how-to-choose- a-good-psychic

Selecting the right spiritual advisor or psychic is much like choosing a doctor. You need to find someone who is good at what they do, empathetic, caring and professional. Ultimately it comes down to your own personal preference. You need to feel comfortable with and have some confidence in whoever you choose.

Just as each doctor has a different bedside manner, each psychic practitioner has a different style. Not only that, the variety of modalities seems endless. There are so many ways to open your Intuition and receive the information that I would need to write a book to simply scratch the surface. However, there are a few basic queues to look for regardless of your preference.

In all professions you will find a wide range of people; those that simply do it for the money, the charlatans, the honest, the ethical and the professional, among others. So what should you look for? What should clue you in that the person you're dealing with isn't totally above board?

Observe the practitioner when they are doing a reading. Do they really listen? Do they seem sincere? Are they more concerned with the time limit and the money than they are with your welfare? Will they simply leave you crying when your time is up, or do they guide you back to a better place?

The question is what kind of state they leave you in. Are they being comforting? If you come across a painful experience, can they help you through it? Having someone see who you really are behind your everyday façade can be a very moving experience. There are times when you will walk away from a reading with tears in your eyes. A good cry is a healthy outlet for your emotions. It can be very cleansing.

Also, you need to remember that we all relate to information through our own filters; our past, our environment, our beliefs, etc. This is a natural human trait. Be aware of that when having a reading. For example, when I was pregnant with my daughter I had several readings; more for advice on my relationship with her father than anything else. A psychic actually suggested I have an abortion, seeing my relationship as basically over. She was so afraid of single motherhood that she could not even conceive of it. She was sincere and trying to be helpful, but that was not good advice for me.

The only way to discover some of these things is to experience them. But, referrals can help. What kinds of things are said about the person? No one is going to be universally adored, so don't write someone off because you hear of one bad experience. We all have bad days; maybe that was one of them. Or the person giving their opinion may not have liked what they were told because it was not what they wanted to hear. I could tell you stories...

There are definite things that should raise red flags for you. You need to be wary of psychics who speak in absolutes. Anyone who claims 100% accuracy is a liar. Scientific studies have shown that even the best of us have 78% to 85% accuracy. A normal person usually rates a 30%.

Be careful of practitioners who throw the word evil around. It is a very powerful word and most of us do not use it lightly. Everyone's heard stories about the kind of psychic who sees evil around you that must be removed, or you will be in great peril and your situation will only worsen. These practitioners will require that you pay them copious amounts of money to remove it. They will usually have you come back for several sessions.

Another variation on this is the psychic

who tries to ride your coattails to success.
I once had to deal with a psychic who
would insert herself into your reading if
she saw any kind of success for you.

What is sad about this type of fraud is that I
have found many of these types to actually
be accurate and gifted psychics. I don't
understand the greed and lust for power
which accompanies this type of behavior.

> Basically, THE PROOF IS IN
> THE PUDDING. Even Jesus
> said *"Be on your guard against*
> *false prophets, who come to*
> *you in sheep's clothing but*
> *underneath are wolves on the*
> *prowl. You will know them by*
> *their deeds."* [Matthew 7:15]

How do you feel after a reading? Was it
uplifting and helpful, or did it foster fear?

Very little of what happens to you is
unavoidable. You need to take
responsibility for your own future. Our
purpose is to give you an idea of the
landscape; you need to decide how you
will navigate it. Blessings.

When working with clients, I share
information and metaphors for self-insight. It
is the responsibility of each person seeking
assistance to be the final determiner of his or

her choices in life. I assume no credit, blame or liability for the impressions I share or any actions that people may take as a result of hearing them. *The point of having a reading is to use the information as a barometer of your path and help you see the bigger picture.* It is not for the psychic to make your decisions for you, but rather to guide you. May your greater good be served.

Blessings, Geralyn

Mahalo! Thank You!

Mahalo for reading my book! I know you could have picked from so many books on this subject. I appreciate that you took a chance on me. Much Mahalo [Great Thanks] for downloading this book and reading it. If you enjoyed it or found it helpful in any way I need your help – please give me a review. This feedback will help me continue to write the kind of book that helps you.

If you love this book and would like more information please let me know :-)

ONE LAST THING... Please take the opportunity to rate and share your thoughts on Facebook and Twitter. If you believe this information is worth sharing, would you please take a few seconds to let your friends know about it? If it turns out to help them, I am sure they will be forever grateful to you. And so will I!

Mahalo & Blessings! Geralyn

Geralyn St Joseph Bio

"A psychic reading from Geralyn St. Joseph is often very specific in detail and always highly transformative. Her information uplifts the spirit and gives one a sense of direction filled with many possibilities. She has helped clients through difficult times by assisting them in discovering the reasons for a seemingly traumatic event."

– Shaman Christopher Ilo

I am a clairvoyant, intuitive reader utilizing a variety of divination tools. I enjoy helping others through my spiritual gifts.

I combine my metaphysical talents with my education to offer different spiritual guidance services; ranging from couple's guidance to business consulting. I have a BA in Communications with concentrations in Law and Psychology.

I have been reading for others since age 11, and have offered my services professionally since 1994. My client base spans the world including India, Japan, Australia and more. I offer my readings and guidance by phone and in- person; and my classes by Internet for my long distance or time challenged clients.

I am a highly effective motivational speaker, delivering talks on various subjects. Seminars and Classes include: Intuitive Tarot, Completing the Circle
– Path to Self-Empowerment, Power of Gemstones, Living from the Heart Series and more!

Blessings! Geralyn St Joseph

I am a spiritual teacher.

That does not mean I think I am better than you.
That does not make me perfect.
That means I do my best to lead by example.
To maintain a clean, close connection with spirit.
That means I try to be patient, understanding and
compassionate.

I have a dark side too.
I acknowledge and embrace it.
I try to use all of my being for good.
I may be loathed by some, that's good.

What I say and the way I live *should* garner a
reaction. Then I know you're listening. Speak out for or
against me and what I do. It does not matter, just start
the discussion, and feel the emotion.

Figure out what *you* stand for.

Be Blessed. Namaste!

Resources

Geralyn St. Joseph
808 261-7866 text or talk
Geralyn@VoiceofSpirit.com

www.WholisticUniversity.org
Meditations & audio for further study
http://wholisticuniversity.blogspot.com/p/practices-for-spiritual-development.html

www.VoiceofSpirit.com — Metaphysical
www.GabrielsTrumpet.net -Intuitive Business Consultant
www.SpiritualParents.com — A Parenting Guide to help you give your children the greatest legacy of all — Love and Wholeness
www.PsychicinHawaii.com — Psychic Geralyn St Joseph and her friends on Oahu
www.HealersinHawaii.com — Energy Healer Geralyn St Joseph and other healers in Hawaii

Blogs
Parenting Blog http://intuitiveparentcoach.blogspot.com/
Metaphysical Blog http://hawaiipsychic.blogspot.com/
Bible Study Blog http://voiceofspirit.blogspot.com/

Geralyn St Joseph has 2 channels on **Blog Talk Radio**:
http://www.blogtalkradio.com/geralynstjoseph
/love--relationships-with-syd--ger

Twitter: @GeralynStJoseph
@KidsHandbook
@SydAndGeralyn

CPSIA information can be obtained
at www.ICGtesting.com
Printed in the USA
FSOW04n2150241217
42710FS